D1721719

For Aria and Anias, may your sibling love inspire positive sibling relationships everywhere. – SA

SIBLING LOVE
Hardcover ISBN 978-1-7346332-3-8
eBook ISBN 978-1-7346332-4-5

Text Copyright © 2020 Sharifa Anozie
Illustrations Copyright © Claudio Espinosa
Developmental Editor: Laura Bontje
Proofreading Editor: Nadara Merrill

All rights reserved. No part of this book may be reproduced in any form, stored in any retrieval system, or transmitted in any formby any means - electronic, mechanical, photocopy, recording, or otherwise - without prior written permission of the publisher.

Published in the United States by The Sacred Word Publishing, a division of The Sacred Word LLC, Los Angeles.

Library of Congress Cataloging-in-Publication Data
Names: Anozie, Sharifa, 1986-author.
Title: Sibling Love / by Sharifa Anozie; art by Claudio Espinosa
Descripction: First Edition. Los Angeles, California: The Sacred Word, [2020] Audience 3-8
Identifiers: LCNN 2020922749 (print) | ISBN 978-1-7346332-3-8
LC record available at https://lccn.loc.gov/2020922749

Printed in China
2020

SIBLING LOVE

by SHARIFA ANOZIE

illustrated by CLAUDIO ESPINOSA

There are many kinds of love in the world.

There's love between friends,
love for your pets,
and the unconditional love
between parents and kids.

But nothing quite compares
to **sibling love.**

It's a lifelong friendship
and an indescribable bond.

Maybe you have a sister,
or your sibling is a big
or little brother.

No matter what kind of siblings you have, what you share is something unique.

Sibling love
is early-morning
hugs and kisses.

It's the way you fall over laughing at each
other's jokes, or how you chase each other
around the yard until you're out of breath.

It's the way you can speak in your own made-up language.

It's pouring syrup all over your pancakes at breakfast,

or getting tangled in a spaghetti mess at dinner time.

It's sharing snacks—

and sometimes not!

Sibling love is singing and dancing together to your favorite songs.

It's family road trips in the car to places far away.

It's fighting over the smallest things, but making up moments later.

Sibling love is how you learn to be fair, gentle, and kind.

It's playing outside, chasing butterflies, and finding slimy bugs.

It's having someone to
snuggle with during
a loud thunderstorm,

and to make sure there are no monsters under the bed.

Sometimes you'll have
different interests and ideas—
and that's okay!

Respect your differences, and celebrate what makes you the same.

Together, you will learn
life's most important lessons.

Some bumps and bruises
will prepare you for the
journey ahead.

When you're having a bad day,
you can count on your siblings
to make it better.

Sibling love is unconditional. It comes from someone who knows you better than anyone else and loves you no matter what.

There are many kinds of
love in the world, but
none quite as special as
sibling love.

ABOUT THE AUTHOR:

Sharifa Anozie
@SHARIFA_ANOZIE

SHARIFA ANOZIE IS A MOTHER, ENTREPRENEUR, AND AUTHOR.

A native New Yorker, her passion for storytelling spans back two decades when she interviewed renowned civil rights advocate, Carolyn Goodman, at just 12 years old. Her poem dedicated to Ms. Goodman traveled the country in The Long Walk to Freedom exhibit and was recognized by some major media outlets. To further both her knowledge and curiosity for stories everywhere, she went on to obtain a journalism degree from Penn State University. As an avid encourager for following your big dreams, Sharifa followed her own by moving across the country in 2012 to pursue a career in entertainment news.

She now lives in Los Angeles with her husband, Jonathan, and their two children.

To find more work from the author visit www.sharifaanozie.com.

ABOUT THE ILLUSTRATOR:

Claudio Espinosa

@KLOHDSTUFF

Claudio Espinosa is a Mexican illustrator and graphic designer who doodles whenever possible and has a big passion for creating fun and whimsical characters. Having worked on diverse projects, from textile design for clothing to backgrounds and character design for animation, he now focuses on illustration for editorial projects, mainly children's books.

To find more work from the illustrator visit www.klohdstuff.com.

CPSIA information can be obtained
at www.ICGtesting.com
Printed in the USA
LVHW070346160621
690290LV00006B/337